A NEW ENGLISH STYLE

TIMELESS INTERIORS BY
SALVESEN GRAHAM

NICOLE SALVESEN
AND MARY GRAHAM

WRITTEN BY
DAVID NICHOLLS

Quadrille

4 FOREWORD
6 INTRODUCTION

14 PIED-À-TERRE
32 WORKING WITH COLOUR
38 COUNTRY ESTATE
66 ARCHITECTURAL DETAILS
72 FLINT HOUSE
94 LAYERING
100 OLD RECTORY
122 DECORATIVE DETAILS
128 MANOR HOUSE
142 COLLECTED & CURATED
148 MOUNTAIN HOME
170 UPSTAIRS DOWNSTAIRS
176 TOWNHOUSE
198 ANTIQUES
204 ARTS & CRAFTS
224 PATTERN
230 GEORGIAN HOUSE
250 THE COLLECTION

254 ACKNOWLEDGEMENTS
256 CREDITS

FOREWORD

When we set up Salvesen Graham in 2013 neither of us imagined that one day in the not-too-distant future we would be adding the finishing touches to a book all about our work. It feels like a huge milestone. And putting it together has reminded us of a series of smaller milestones along the way: our first big country house project; our first project overseas; the development of our own homeware collection. What a lovely trip down memory lane.

It was around the time leading up to Salvesen Graham's 10th anniversary that we were asked to create this book. Immediately our minds were whirring with ideas – with possibilities. One thing we knew fairly early on was that we wanted the book to share some of the qualities of the interiors' schemes that we create for our clients: to be beautiful but also useful, something that feels special today but will still be relevant in 20 years' time. It's not for us to say if we've achieved that but we hope that we have.

We've discovered that working on a book is, in many ways, like any other creative project. It's exciting, stimulating and fun; there are challenges that require solutions; it is an opportunity to learn new things. We are firm believers that the most successful endeavours are the result of brilliant collaborations and so this was a chance to bring in the expertise of other specialists in their field.

One of these is David Nicholls, the long-time deputy editor of *House & Garden* magazine and a friend. David wrote the first article about us many years ago and he has encouraged and championed us ever since. It felt like we were coming full circle when we asked him to write the book and it has been so much fun working on it with him.

Putting together this collection of projects and committing some of our ideas to print has been an incredibly special process. And an emotional one: we've been able to step back and take stock, to see how far we've come and maybe even give ourselves some ideas for where to go next.

We give an awful lot of ourselves to our work and this book is something to show our friends and families too, to say: 'This is what we do. This is why we missed that concert or party or mentioned the odd sleepless night. This is why we spent so much of that holiday taking pictures of doors, windows and close-ups of hinges.'

We're incredibly proud of how far we've come and of this body of work that marks the first chapter of Salvesen Graham. And of course, we wouldn't have a book at all if it weren't for our brilliant team – past and present. One of our great sources of pride is creating a happy and creative studio to work in.

Special thanks, too, to our clients who trusted us, pushed us, collaborated with us, and who have allowed us to show off our work in their homes.

Nicole and Mary
Nicole Salvesen and Mary Graham

INTRODUCTION

It was early 2016 when I first met Mary and Nicole at an industry event in a smart hotel in South Kensington and we immediately hit it off. In relative terms they were new kids on the block: full of ambition and enthusiasm and completely charming. A few months later I was at a photoshoot for a magazine article I was writing about one of their projects. I don't think I realised it at the time but it was their first big piece of editorial coverage. What a lovely moment to have shared with them – and we've shared many others since. There have been plenty more parties, of course (this is a business that loves to celebrate itself), but I've also had the opportunity to visit several of their interior design projects – in the countryside and the city; houses created for clients; homes they have made for themselves. I've had a front row seat to watch their remarkable progression.

As I have got to know them, I've seen that, like the best creatives, Mary and Nicole share an insatiable sense of curiosity. It is a quality they bring to their lives as designers too. They both grew up spending weekends vising England's great country houses and continue to do so today: Chatsworth House ('grand but comfortable'), Syon Park ('Adam's detailing is a constant source of inspiration') and Dyrham Park ('it has the loveliest pantry lined in Delft tiles'). Their interests have led them to investigate 18th-century architecture on the other side of the Atlantic too ('Georgian architecture with a Charleston slant is something so particular'). Both are avid collectors of books on historic decorative details. They attend the talks and seminars; they give the talks and seminars. 'We never stop learning,' Nicole said during one of our interviews. 'There are always problems to solve, solutions to find or references to discover to help give us the confidence to know: This can be done. This has been done.'

The pair met long before they set up Salvesen Graham in 2013. Although they both went to Durham University (where Nicole studied theology, sociology and anthropology and Mary studied history) they didn't become firm friends until a few years after graduating. By then they had gravitated to London and, like so many young graduates, had tried their hands in various jobs in the creative industries. Separately they hit upon interior design as something they were interested in pursuing and each took courses at the KLC School of Design.

One of Nicole's first mentors was the international design legend Nina Campbell. In her early career, Nina was an assistant to John Fowler: 'I considered myself lucky

just to be carrying his bag,' she once told me. Nicole is equally grateful for the time she worked for Nina: 'I learned so much, but perhaps more than anything it was simply to roll your sleeves up and get stuck into any job. I am the hands-on designer I am today because of that experience.' Mary's formative years were spent working for Cindy Leveson, a stalwart of the English interiors scene who has been decorating significant country houses across the land for over 30 years (the most famous of these includes ongoing projects at Goodwood House). 'Cindy was always so generous in exposing me to the incredible interiors that she was helping to preserve and bring back to life and reinvigorate,' Mary recalls. 'She taught me the essence of the English country house at its grandest and also how to distill that idea and apply it anywhere.'

In their early years of navigating the world of interior design the two became valuable sounding boards and confidantes, bonding over a shared ambition to master the elements of traditional English decorating, and to move it forward. Nicole and Mary are part of a generation of designers who came up at a time when the likes of Robert Kime, Nicky Haslam and David Mlinaric were still in their pomp. And while there is a gradual but unstoppable changing of the guard under way, the lessons of who and what have gone before are being explored, teased out and developed by the likes of Mary and Nicole and their contemporaries.

At the time of writing, it is just over a decade since Mary and Nicole decided to make the leap and start their own interior design studio. As they explained in the Foreword, this book is a chance to reflect on that period. When they told me that they had been approached about doing a book on their work, I hoped that they would ask me to write it. It is more than a portfolio of their work. So many of our conversations were centred around the ideas that shape classic English decorating and the country house style: the decorative and architectural details, the erosion of the boundary between formal rooms and back-of-house spaces, the role of colour and pattern, of antiques and art. They were as keen to talk about their influences and the foundations of their work as they were about the projects themselves. It meant some wonderful digressions about jib doors, nib walls and more.

The premise of this book is simple: Nicole Salvesen and Mary Graham are interior designers whose work is a modern expression of classic English decorating; they are part of a new wave of designers helping to evolve the idea of the 'English country house style'. Because despite its familiar and appealing conventions (layered fabrics; capacious, squishy sofas; artfully, playfully curated spaces, etc.), it is not a look that is set in aspic. To work in this tradition is not to recreate set pieces established by the great decorators and houses of the past. As I hope the following pages will illustrate, it is a balancing act: taking the best of what has come before and making it feel fresh for life in the 21st century. The book is structured in a way that attempts to show how Salvesen Graham does just that.

We'll take a deep dive into nine of Mary and Nicole's projects: houses big and small, and a pied-à-terre or two. It will take us on a tour of the English countryside, into the heart of London and on a trip across the Atlantic. One thing I have noticed when looking at these houses all together is how the English country house style can be adapted: dialled up or down, made crisp and tailored or pleasingly dishevelled. It can feel deeply traditional or have a clear sense of modernity. It can even have an American accent. I think that is one of the things that I most admire about Mary and Nicole's work: they have an incredibly clear idea of who they are as designers and of the tradition that they are working within, but they are able to adapt that in a way that reflects place, person and circumstance.

Interspersed between these chapters is a series of short essays which, for the most part, consider different aspects of English decorating. The essays have given me an opportunity to look at how Mary and Nicole's work fits within this aesthetic and to discuss their points of view on various subjects. There's a bit of historical context, a few examples from their projects and lots of ideas and things to think about for anyone embarking on their own interior design endeavours. While this book isn't a 'how-to', it has been conceived as a guide to some of the key elements of English decorating. And alongside each of these essays we'll also hear directly from Mary and Nicole with their personal insights and experiences.

One of the things I hope this book conveys is how bright and fun Mary and Nicole are. They are easy company, generous with their ideas and as warm as the interiors they create. I wasn't a bit surprised when a client of theirs told me that she was thinking of putting her house on the market and buying a new one just so she could relive the experience of working with them. She may have been laughing, but I wasn't completely convinced she was joking.

PIED-À-TERRE

Turnkey property. Few word pairings will have a more chilling effect on the heart of anyone interested in the idea of creating a space that feels like home. It smacks of convenience and anonymity; of soulless interiors designed to perform a function; something closer to a financial rather than an emotional investment.

But it doesn't have to be that way, as can be seen in this apartment that takes up the top two floors of a 1920s' mansion block in London's Mayfair. It is a wonderful example of how designers can create a complete home from scratch in a way that feels authentic, right down to the books on the shelves and the martini glasses in the cabinet.

The owners of the apartment are an American couple based in North Carolina who have a young daughter; they bought it as a pied-à-terre. London is a city they love; they were married there and visit regularly. The apartment had been bashed about over the years and had evolved into what Mary describes as 'a 1990s' atrocity'. These things happen.

As with a few of the projects in this book, the design stages of this one coincided with the darkest days of the pandemic. Perhaps that's why the client ended up being more involved in the process than she might otherwise have been. It certainly played a role in the final aesthetic. Lockdowns meant that we all had more time to think about our homes and how they might be improved. And while the client initially had a few reservations about some of Nicole and Mary's more exuberant decorative inclinations, she had something of an epiphany.

'The world is miserable right now,' the client emailed. 'I want this apartment to convey a sense of joy.' What could be more joyous than opening the door to your home and being greeted by a light-filled space hung with a glowing, golden, hand-painted silk wall covering? Its selection was one of the last decisions to be made and it makes the most wonderful first impression.

Although the scale of the apartment doesn't compare to the houses in this book, it wouldn't be completely accurate to describe it as a small project. It required a huge amount of floorplan reordering and rationalising, with staircases removed and new ones installed, walls taken out and new ones put elsewhere. One of the most impactful interventions was the creation of a large and glamorous foyer, like something you might find in a New York apartment rather than an Edwardian mansion block.

'There's no point having a pied-à-terre if it ends up looking like a hotel,' Nicole says. 'You want to be instantly at home in the space, and for it to reflect the city it's in; otherwise you could be anywhere.'

On the main floor they turned a clutter of three rooms into one large living space which is a great example in how to give structure and harmony to an open space that needs to perform multiple functions. Where a sofa backs onto a leather-topped desk, a sitting room becomes a place to work. Moving along the room there is another demarcation, as an upholstered banquette at a dining table is nestled against a kitchen island. Along one wall, a Georgian cabinet, club fender and built-in dresser form an interesting, undulating rhythm. Opposite, the windows are curtained rather than dressed with blinds, while all of the walls are covered in grass cloth. These aren't obvious choices for a space that is part kitchen, but they add to the cohesive quality of the room.

With the help of an art advisor that Nicole and Mary often work with, a collection of works by British artists was created from scratch. And it is very believably curated, as though amassed over years with 'good' pieces mixed in with inexpensive ones that might have been bought on a whim. Not every wall has a showstopper.

The shelves in the main bedroom are lined with books by British authors or have a British subject matter. 'Readable books rather than just ones that sit on a shelf as a display,' says Mary. She is particularly satisfied to hear that the clients are gradually working their way through them. Here, the walls are covered in a hand-painted de Gournay chinoiserie and behind a jib door is an en suite bathroom with an extremely joyous detail. Here and there, the walls of the bathroom have been hand-painted by one of de Gournay's artists with some of the motifs from the wallpaper in the bedroom.

ABOVE: Despite being a relatively small home, it has an airy and spacious feel, in no small part thanks to the double height entrance hall that Salvesen Graham created with stairs leading up to the roof terrace (page 17). PREVIOUS PAGE: In a large open space, careful placement of furniture creates comfortable, rational 'zones'.

ABOVE and RIGHT: Just off this open-plan living space is a prep kitchen-cum-utility room which is tucked away behind a pocket door. It's perfect for keeping clutter out of sight when the clients are entertaining.

PREVIOUS, LEFT and ABOVE: A tailored half-tester above the bed and a handpainted de Gournay wallcovering gives the bedroom a luxuriant feel, while jib doors conceal wardrobes and an en suite bathroom.

ABOVE and RIGHT: Grosgrain ribbon used around the edges of the walls adds a decorative detail as well as a sense of architectural structure to the guest room and connected bathroom.

ABOVE and LEFT: A tiny little 'cabin' room at the top of the building which looks out onto the terrace. The bespoke carpet has the same pattern of the Salvesen Graham Zig Zag fabric used for the blinds and on the walls.

PIED-À-TERRE

WORKING WITH COLOUR

In many ways it is the country houses of the 18th century that established what 'English decorating' has come to mean today. This is true not least in the role that colour plays within the tradition. The Georgians could never be accused of having been shy with colour, favouring, at different times, pastel shades and more vibrant hues, often grounded with a mixture of stony whites and earthy tones. Succeeding generations tweaked the palette, adding to it and refining it, which culminated in a colour language that is as much about mood as it is about a particular shade.

The same could be said for the homes created by Nicole and Mary, whose work is so rooted in this tradition and is often described as 'colourful'. But perhaps that word is a little misleading, conjuring images of bright technicolour spaces and unexpected juxtapositions. As the pages of this book will attest, quite the opposite is true. 'It is possible to be colourful without being overly bold,' explains Mary. 'And we are evangelical about the idea of being colourful without being "wacky".'

Just like the decorating greats that preceded and continue to inspire them, their aim is to craft a feeling of harmony. That is the somewhat magic quality that colour has the power to create. As the great American decorator Elsie de Wolfe once wrote: 'Color should be treated kindly, but it should never be allowed to get the best of a house or room. And it must be taught to respect the feelings of those who must live with it.'

They are advocates of telling a colour story throughout a house without colour becoming the story of the house. 'We often start a scheme with what we refer to as a "hero fabric",' explains Mary. It might be an antique suzani that the client already owns and loves, or a fabric that the designers have suggested. 'We can build an entire scheme using the colours from that fabric. It can take us down so many different avenues.' For example, the shades used on the branches and leaves, flowers and fauna of a tree of life fabric can be extrapolated and amplified when deciding on curtains and cushions, paint colours and decorative accessories. In the drawing room of one Salvesen Graham project, the exact colours in a chinoiserie wallcovering were repeated in the trim used on the leading edge of the curtains. It is incredible how something so subtle can really contribute to the cohesion of a room.

'In reality you don't need to have an extensive palette of colours in a house because the same colour will appear completely differently in different rooms,' Nicole says. A hallway usually has less natural light than a drawing room, and that will impact how a colour is perceived. The light in a north-facing room will affect colour in a very different way to a south-facing room. 'We like to celebrate the nuance of the same colour and how it can change naturally in different places,' Mary agrees.

Do they have any hard and fast rules when it comes to what colours they will always or never use? Not particularly, although the keen-eyed will spot an affinity with greeny-blues and flashes of raspberry. 'What we don't do is try to change the character of a space with colour. You can't enforce a style or aesthetic onto a room or a home', explains Nicole. As with so much of their work, it's about taking a sympathetic approach; one that feels comfortable.

MY COLOUR JOURNEY

Since I was a child I have filled my life with colour. But while I instinctively know how colour makes me feel, one thing I had to learn was how important the environment is when choosing colour. Or rather, the intensity or tone of the colour.

The eye needs different things when entering a house in the city as opposed to the countryside, the seaside or the mountains. That is perhaps something more soothing to take the edge off an urban environment; fun and bright to keep up the energy of a beach house; a little earthier in a wooded glade.

When putting together a colour palette, I encourage others to consider that the colour journey starts from outside the house.

NICOLE SALVESEN

COUNTRY ESTATE

Trewithen is one of Cornwall's finest houses, and its saloon is without doubt its most impressive room – a meeting of Palladian symmetry and exuberant Rococo detailing. The largest room in the house, the saloon is organised around a central fireplace with cross-vaulted screens on each end and doors leading out onto the garden. It is a confection of a space: painted powder pink with decorative plasterwork picked out in white. The sofas and armchairs are generously stuffed and look squishy and inviting. It is an illustration of the care and focus it has taken to bring this historic house to the latest stage in its evolution, namely the commitment of its owners and the team of professionals that they assembled to pull it off. To fully appreciate this, it's helpful to understand the context.

The destruction of Britain's architectural heritage, and in particular the loss of so many of its great country houses, is well documented. It is still shocking to read, however, that in 1955 one country house was being demolished in England every week. Simply put, societal and financial upheaval and two world wars contrived to make it impossible for many of the landed gentry to maintain their historic estates.

That is in part what makes Trewithen so special. Its story dates back to the early 18th century when its first iteration was built by the architect Thomas Edwards for an attorney named Philip Hawkins. Three hundred years later, the house and its 29 acres of wooded parkland remain in the hands of Hawkins' descendants. A huge sense of responsibility comes with inheriting a house like this: the owners wanted to make it right for the next 100 years. It must be difficult not to feel under a certain degree of scrutiny when the walls of your home are hung with the painted portraits of your ancestors.

First though, it had to be right for them and their young family. Trewithen is a Grade I listed building which means it is subject to strict legal protections. The owners gathered a team that included Salvesen Graham, the architect Martin Llewellyn and the architectural and landscape historian Timothy Mowl, who wrote a heritage report providing vital arguments for some of the changes that would be made. Together with a host of local specialists and craftspeople, their aim was to coax the house into the 21st century.

Like many surviving country estates, Trewithen has long opened its doors to visitors. Sam, who grew up at Trewithen, was well used to sharing his home with those drawn to its magnificent collection of camellias and woodland walks, its paintings, books and ceramics. His family lived primarily in one part of the house while the rest was for the touring public. But that was to change. Trewithen would remain open to the public for part of the year, but he and Kitty wanted their family to use the full width of the house.

A reordering was needed, particularly on the ground floor where rooms swapped places and changed function. Most significantly, the kitchen went back to its historic home (it had been a sitting room for 40 years), making space for a boot room, utility room and pantry in a less protected 1980s extension. 'The first six months were spent going over floor plans again and again with the architect,' recalls Mary. Today there is an easy flow between this hardworking part of the house, and the adjoining breakfast room, playroom and smoking room. The latter is now a cosy sitting room – the perfect spot for having supper on a tray watching television. This was in fact part of the brief.

Above all, what Nicole and Mary have brought to Trewithen is the warmth, friendliness and ease that the family wanted their home to exude. Of course, a house like this will always have a sense of formality to it; how could it not? The dining room, saloon and library are still highlights of the tours: they are each wonderful spaces. But one would never get the sense of a velvet rope just out of sight. When the last visitors leave, they are family spaces. And that is crucial in a historic house like Trewithen; because if no one actually wants to live there, you're left with little more than a museum.

ABOVE and RIGHT: The joyful, bright yellow flower room was created as a foil to the more neutral tones in the back of house areas where beautiful yet practical joinery was carefully designed to sit comfortably in this historic house.

PREVIOUS and LEFT: Just off the kitchen (overleaf) is a breakfast room that was once a series of smaller spaces. The yellow and white coffered ceiling, check curtains and wallcovering create a more relaxed alternative to the dining room (above).

COUNTRY ESTATE

LEFT and ABOVE: Glossy blue walls and a blousy chintz feature in one of the studies, while walls in the 'smoking room' were covered in green velvet. The saloon (overleaf) is a confection in pink.

COUNTRY ESTATE

'Formality doesn't have to mean uncomfortable. Even the grandest rooms should be somewhere that the whole family can use and enjoy.'

MARY GRAHAM

ABOVE and LEFT: The way fabric is used when dressing a bed can dramatically affect the look and feel of a space. The relaxed box pleats featured on the left give a casual country house feel, whereas the more tailored approach above (inspired by the work of Veere Grenney) wouldn't look out of place in the city.

COUNTRY ESTATE

'A more neutral backdrop with uncluttered architectural detailing and a textured wall covering add a sense of restraint and calm in a room with plenty of patterned fabrics and trimmings.'

NICOLE SALVESEN

COUNTRY ESTATE

ABOVE and LEFT: The impressive bathroom (connected to the main bedroom), and this spare bedroom, are examples of the 'handsome floral' look that Salvesen Graham is so adept at creating.

ABOVE, LEFT and OVERLEAF: *These two rooms were reconfigured by Salvesen Graham to make the most of the view over the historic garden. They moved doors and created a new bathroom while being sensitive to the age and significance of the house.*

COUNTRY ESTATE

ARCHITECTURAL DETAILS

If you were to look at an interior designed by Salvesen Graham, you might initially be struck by the way that pattern and colour dance across a room. As with so many aspects of life however, when you look past that which at first demands your attention, you may discover a layer that has its own story to tell.

Is there an architrave around the door, and if so, is it quite simple or more expressive? When does a doorway need to announce its presence and when should it disappear from sight altogether? These are the sorts of questions Salvesen Graham might ponder at the very earliest stage of devising the scheme for a room. As designers they are firm advocates for the architectural detailing that Adolf Loos argued against in his infamous 1908 manifesto, *Ornament & Crime*.

'To describe architectural details in a home simply as "ornaments" makes them sound like a finishing point,' says Nicole. 'But they are so integral to the look and feel of a room that for us they are the starting point. We make sure we spend time with our clients discussing the importance of the bones and getting those right.' That can include a curved piece of joinery that gently encourages the eye to move in a particular direction, a trick-of-the-eye arrangement of tiles that gives the impression of panelling, or a polished brass trim to give structure to a ceiling.

British homes have a rich history of architectural details because so much of the country's housing stock comes from a time before the more restrained fashions of modernism and the privations of post-war life. There remain significant numbers of Georgian houses in England, and there is certainly no shortage of Victorian ones. These are the homes in which Nicole and Mary grew up and where they cut their teeth as young designers.

The designers' interest in the minutiae of architectural detailing can take them anywhere from the British Library to a tour of a 19th-century château in rural France. It is all information gathering to see how Soane or Nash or Devereux might have done things. But Mary and Nicole apply this knowledge with a confidence that allows them to adapt what has gone before them in a way that is right for the project.

Understanding historic houses is to appreciate the appropriateness of a cornice or the depth of a skirting board. It is to know if a piece of joinery should be adorned with beading, and whether it should be plain, Greek key or Vitruvian scroll. Understanding life, however, is to appreciate that homes are not static spaces – they evolve over time. As such, Nicole and Mary work with a sense of judiciousness rather than a slavishness to the past.

Elsewhere, Salvesen Graham will disregard tradition altogether and do something that simply looks lovely. Being anachronistic works best when it is done from a place of knowledge: a sort of informed rebellion. As rebellions go, a scalloped edge is admittedly a fairly gentle one; it is safe to say these did not play a large role in the original joinery of many boot rooms in Georgian manor houses. It is also obvious that their inclusion in the 21st century-iteration of that space can provide a fleeting and almost subconscious moment of delight.

A VISIT TO CHARLESTON

Nicole and I had an epiphany on a trip to Charleston, South Carolina, a city rich in Georgian architecture. The houses we visited, including Nathanial Russell House and Drayton Hall, were familiar in many ways, but they had architectural details that were so distinct to the time and place in which they were built. They had a slightly more stylistically naive aspect to them but they were still beautiful.

This made us realise how varied and exportable and transferable these classical details are. The purest expression of a Greek key can be dialled up or down, made crisp and perfect or a little rough around the edges; both are completely valid. This kind of flexibility is what ensures that no two interiors will be the same. Seeing these houses really crystallised that for us.

MARY GRAHAM

FLINT HOUSE

An Edwardian vicarage in a picturesque West Sussex hamlet is the setting for this holiday home belonging to a young London-based family. The clients have a more modern, architecturally led home in the city and wanted somewhere they could escape to and invite friends for a quintessentially English weekend in the country.

The house is typical of its age and location: neat and pretty but sturdy-looking; flint-clad with brick detailing and white painted gables. In the 1980s, its size nearly doubled thanks to a large two-floor extension at the back. 'It had been a family house for a long time and had a lovely feel,' Mary recalls. 'That's so important. Even if you completely change a house, its feeling will remain, as though it's part of the building's DNA'.

Now reimagined, reordered and redecorated, the house is perfect for how the family wanted to spend time there, and for all the hosting and entertaining. Flexible spaces were high on their wish list. The main living area, for example, is a double reception room that could easily have remained a large drawing room. Instead, it is a multifunctional, adaptable space where, at one end, a round table piled with books can extend into a dining table for 12. At the other is a comfortable sitting area where blousy chintz sofas sit beneath contemporary art. There is a card table in one window, while two armchairs huddle conspiratorially in another. 'On a rainy day you could have a few sets of people doing their own thing and they wouldn't be on top of each other,' Mary says.

'We run through a lot of scenarios in our head when we are designing a room,' Nicole explains. 'How would it work at Christmas or for a party? Where would your elderly relative sit if they wanted to be with the family without being in the midst of the action?' It is incredibly considered spatial design.' Another example of this can be found across the hall in the study, a handsome space decorated in rich autumnal tones. It is necessarily cosy and quiet; a place to concentrate. But fold open its half-glazed double doors and it transforms into a more expansive room, with the bookcase in the hallway now acting as its fourth wall. It's very clever.

A newly decorated weekend house can, by its nature, take time to fill with the ephemera of life and to have the edges knocked off it in a way that feels lived in. Then again, that roughed-up, slightly shabby take on English decorating isn't for everyone. The owners of this house wanted a fresh take on the country house style. 'They were delighted to embrace chintz and florals and antiques,' Mary recalls. 'But their taste is a bit more tailored and pared back. That's one thing we've been happy to show clients: that you can still get elements of this traditional English look even if you don't live in a dishevelled country house with piles of books everywhere.' What Salvesen Graham have delivered is a happy meeting place between the traditional and the modern: a freshly scrubbed and polished version of the country house style.

In the kitchen, the practicality of a run of fitted units is offset by the inclusion of freestanding pieces that have a more farmhouse feel: an enormous prep-table-cum-island with attractive turned wood legs; a bespoke but antique-looking breakfast cabinet in a rich mid-tone wood. Mary and Nicole designed the Dutch-style, glass-fronted cabinet to hide the enormous fridge freezer the house needed, which would have otherwise added an unfortunate industrial element to the space.

The bedrooms upstairs are decorated in a way in which guests can be in no doubt they are waking up in an English country house. One room is decorated in the iconic Bowood fabric by Colefax & Fowler. The daughters' bedroom is equally exuberant: a classic chintz has been paperbacked and hung on the walls, used for the valance and canopy of the beds, the curtains and to cover a skirted armchair. It has a wonderful fairytale quality to it.

'A weekend house is for fun times and making memories,' Nicole says. 'So, it's nice to add a bit of theatre.' The main bedroom has a wall of cupboards where one of the doors opens onto an enormous bathroom. 'It's like a secret room – something magic.' Similarly, the walls of the children's loo downstairs are hand-painted with scenes from *The Wind in the Willows*.

'We always try to make room for the unexpected. That might mean adding something like a pretty patterned wallpaper to those utilitarian, back-of-house spaces.'

MARY GRAHAM

ABOVE and LEFT: A combination of wood and stone is used in different ways throughout a large open space to give a distinct feel to different 'zones' and to help ease the transition between the original house and a modern extension.

'Modern life means we often use rooms in old houses in new ways: a library can be a perfectly lovely dining room and vice versa. This is one of the ways homes with history can evolve with each generation.'

NICOLE SALVESEN

ABOVE and RIGHT: The dining table and seating area are all part of one large, flexible space – part drawing room, part dining room-cum-library – perfect for weekend entertaining.

LEFT: The guest rooms and bathrooms show some of the ways the look can be subtly updated with fresh, modern colours and unexpected elements, such as a Swedish rug. ABOVE: The doors to the en suite bathroom are disguised to look like cupboard doors, creating a delightful 'reveal' when opened.

ABOVE: A bedroom, completely swathed in the classic Bowood fabric by Colefax & Fowler, embodies the best of classic English country house style. RIGHT: A bedroom where a single chintz fabric has been used on walls, furniture and curtains, creating a quintessentially English look.

LEFT: The client had always dreamed of the perfect children's bedroom, which has been realised here through the use of a repeating classic chintz and layering with traditional elements, such as the eiderdown and patchwork cushions on the bed. ABOVE: This cheerful bathroom adjoins the twin bedroom.

LAYERING

'How do you feel in a room where everything is brand new?,' Nicole asks. 'You feel as though you can't touch anything and you're afraid to sit down. You don't want that feeling in any space, but especially not in your home.' Such one-note decorating is a mystery to Salvesen Graham, and there is one quality that is most associated with their work: that of a 'layered' interior.

When many of us consider what this might look like, our minds naturally turn to patterned textiles and their myriad combinations: chintzes, florals and stripes on sofas, cushions, curtains, club fenders and carpets. While for many decorators, this is the very definition of 'layered', for Salvesen Graham it is but one aspect. Mary and Nicole take a holistic approach to layering an interior, which is all about balancing the combinations of hard materials (the stone and the wood), the finishes (the polished, the burnished, the glossy, the matt) and the motifs (the classical with the modern, the domestic with the global). These all conspire to create the delectable millefeuille effect of these carefully considered spaces.

There is a pleasing irony in the fact that, at their best, these meticulously planned spaces feel as though they have simply 'happened'. They do not feel overdesigned or self-conscious or bear the fingerprints of the interior designer. And that's because the inspirations for this aesthetic come from rooms that were genuinely created over a lifetime, or longer.

The roots of the very layered, English country house look can be found in a time when a home spoke of generations past; of ancestors who filled rooms with furniture they found comfortable and walls with art they deemed beautiful. Proceeding generations inherited what were now 'antiques', and then added their own layer, which would in turn become their descendants' antiques. They went on grand tours and brought back their discoveries and influences. The tendrils of Empire reached out and returned with 'exotic' objects and ideas that found their way into the drawing rooms of the gentry.

These spaces weren't rushed; they evolved over time. The challenge for Salvesen Graham is to capture the spirit of this evolution in a way that feels natural.

'Layering is the thing that turns the two-dimensional into the three-dimensional,' explains Mary. Perhaps this extra dimension is a feeling – of comfort. 'A room will feel complete when we finish and hand it over to a client,' explains Nicole. 'But it's so important that there is still space for it to evolve after that point.' One of the keys to this is that you want to be able to move something and for the scheme not to fall apart because it's so precise and planned.

The beauty of something that is layered well is that you can live in it and adjust and adapt and it still feels good. Robert Harling, the founding editor of British *House & Garden*, once wrote: 'Most of us want a sitting room which, on entering for the first or thousandth time, evokes a sense of visual pleasure plus a prospect of relaxation.' Who could want anything more?

IS A ROOM EVER FINISHED?

I learned from watching my mother that a room is never really finished. To this day she will change things around, add something or rearrange what's there to create a slightly different feeling. It taught me that rooms are meant to evolve.

It's important to have the space — the physical space and the headspace — to find and place something you love. When I finish working on a project for a client, a room will feel complete, but the truth is, this is just the first incarnation of the room. I'm handing over the baton for them to add their own layers in time. A well-decorated room is one that accommodates these changes and will allow for an evolution without having to completely redecorate.

NICOLE SALVESEN

OLD RECTORY

The migration from city to countryside is not an unusual one for couples once children come into the frame. That was the situation the owners of this early 19th-century vicarage in a bucolic spot in the south-east of England found themselves in a number of years ago. In fact, the husband had grown up in the house and he wanted his memory of it being a happy family home to be continued for his own children. He and his wife were young entrepreneurs, fresh from London and wanting a clean, modern take on the English country house style. This would be realised spatially as well as decoratively.

First though, there would be some reconfiguring of the 'slightly higgledy piggledy' layout, most significantly doing away with one of the three staircases connecting the ground and first floor. This created substantial extra usable space on both floors, and in each case it was a dramatic improvement.

If Salvesen Graham has a signature detail in spatial design, it might be the use of a nib wall. Extending perhaps an arm length into a room, a nib wall gives the suggestion rather than the reality of a partition. Two of them will create a slightly pinched shape within a large open-plan space. 'People have become so accustomed to the idea of the all-in-one kitchen and living room and it's hard to let go of this,' Nicole explains. 'It's appealing for young families who want to be altogether, or parents who need to keep an eye on the children while they prepare dinner. But families and lifestyles evolve, and open-plan might not always be the right answer.'

In this case, the client got the best of both worlds: a vast kitchen, dining and living area partially separated with glazed nib walls. The decoration is crisp and fresh with a palette of cream and khaki, red, pink and yellow. And there was plenty of room left for the client to express herself with prints, paintings and decorative plates. This is a really joyful family space, now connected to a newly created terrace with the addition of double doors leading out into the garden.

It is quite feminine, which can, in some ways, also be said for the rest of the decoration in the house. 'She is an incredibly impressive businesswoman and very straight talking,' Nicole says. 'She is also very feminine. She wanted the opposite of stuffy and old-fashioned.' That said, Salvesen Graham retained some of the most handsome and useful antiques that were already in the house. 'In a country house it's often the antiques that ground a room,' Mary explains. 'They add history and depth and, in a way, integrity to a space. It wouldn't feel English without them. It would feel as though something were missing.'

As such, the pretty pink panelled drawing room is anchored by a handsome secretaire and long case clock. Likewise, the dining room maintains two useful demilune tables, while the long mahogany dining table wears a long fringed tablecloth most of the year. A marble-topped sideboard is painted glossy red, adding a glamorous but slightly anachronistic touch. Well chosen pieces, some of them newly acquired, also pepper the scheme of the master suite upstairs—an interconnected bedroom, dressing room and bathroom—made possible by the removal of that staircase.

Something that Nicole and Mary believe in deeply is leaving their clients with a home that will continue to work for the next steps in their life. 'It's our job to help clients think a little more long-term,' Mary explains. 'It can be daunting thinking about a children's bedroom needing space do homework when they're still in nappies. But those are the kinds of conversations that we bring up, particularly when people are taking on their first big project.' This old vicarage has been designed with plenty of room to continue evolving and adapting as the needs of the family change.

There are playful elements too. The downstairs loo is joyfully decorated with squiggles and spots wallpaper teamed with apple-green painted woodwork. The fireplace and joinery in the study have been painted a vibrant teal. Armchairs and sofas wear frilly skirts, while a collection of vibrantly coloured vintage insect prints creates a reason to stop and smile in the back hallway. It all feels so right in a house that is starting to build new memories as a happy family home.

ABOVE and LEFT: In the hallway, some framed entomology prints in bright colours, and bold blue-painted woodwork in the study, help give this house a fun and lighthearted feel.

ABOVE and RIGHT: The kitchen is intentionally a serene space; its walls and joinery are painted the same mellow shade with linen blinds to match, while the pantry next door (previous page) is a gentle sage green.

'Clever joinery can hide a multitude of sins, but it can be a light touch addition to a room, with decorative detailing and a loose, unfitted feel.'

MARY GRAHAM

ABOVE and RIGHT: The colour green runs through the house, from a pretty lichen in the boot room, to bold arsenic in the downstairs loo, with a dash of deep olive green on the kitchen chairs (previous page).

ABOVE and LEFT: Responding to a common client concern about the use of too much 'brown furniture' in a room, Salvesen Graham cleverly covered the mahogany dining table with a bespoke fringed cloth and painted a sideboard in a vibrant raspberry high gloss.

ABOVE and RIGHT: A fresh colour palette and a curation of characterful decorative accessories gives the sitting room, with newly added panelling and some inherited antiques, a fresh feel.

ABOVE and LEFT: A spare bedroom was sacrificed to create a larger master suite that includes a bedroom, two dressing rooms and a dual aspect bathroom bathed in light. It is a luxurious use of space and a great place to retreat to when there is a house full of guests.

'We are enormous fans of a clothed table, particularly if it has a trim: it is a brilliant tool to soften a space and a way to introduce another fabric.'

NICOLE SALVESEN

DECORATIVE DETAILS

Perhaps more than any other, decorative details are a subject at the very heart of classic English decorating (even the ones that were imported from continental Europe). Individually they delight the eye, add elements of interest and elevate the otherwise plain. Collectively they form the rich tapestry of the layered interior. They have the power to make a room feel the way it feels: complete, balanced, lovely. And they are a key tool in the armoury that Nicole and Mary use in every project they design.

Decorative details define the world of passementerie and fabric, specialist finishes, murals and trompe l'oeil, of the myriad options for curtains and blinds and ways to dress a bed. It is arguably interior design at its most artistic and it carves out a space for the delightful in a room. 'But, like so much of what we do, it comes down to that fusion between decoration and practicality,' explains Mary. 'I think that's why the details don't feel frivolous – because there is a reason behind them. The joy is that they also look really lovely.' To hear them discuss the decorative devices that they employ is to hear about how they might also provide an architectural benefit, a place to focus or a way of distracting, a trick of the eye or covering something or providing balance.

Take, for example, the way that several of the rooms in this book are framed with a ribbon or braided trim or border, an idea that goes back to the 18th century before being given a more modern but very English spin by David Hicks in the 1960s. In some places the trim might be in a colour that contrasts with the wall; in other cases it might be the subtlest variation of the same hue. While the effect is very different, in both cases it will serve the practical purpose of covering a junction, for example where a wall meets a cornice or skirting board or where a chimneypiece nestles into its opening. 'It would always have been used if the walls were lined in fabric, to conceal the raw edge of the fabric,' says Nicole. 'But even if the walls are painted or wallpapered, it will give it a really finished look.'

What is unknowable, if you aren't an interior designer, is the level of detail and the number of decisions that go into creating a scheme that is rich in decorative details. With lampshades, some will be gathered while others are flat. Some cushions at the back might just have piping while the showstopper at the front has a special trim. Upholstered furniture: will there be double piping, single piping, gimp braid or nailing? The legs on a piece of furniture: are they visible or covered with a skirt or bullion fringe. And, crucially, how do all of these elements work together? It could so easily become discordant, to conceal a lack of sophistication with high drama and theatricality. Nicole and Mary's goal, however, is to create a sense of harmony. 'What we don't want is something gimmicky or something obvious,' Nicole insists.

How they achieve this is through restraint and an understanding of hierarchy. And by that, they don't mean that the primary or 'important' rooms of a house are the ones lavished with more decorative detailing. 'It's more an understanding that not all rooms need to have the same level of detailing,' she continues. As Mary puts it: 'a detail ceases to be a detail if it's everywhere. It's far more interesting when you see it in moments. It's more special.'

WHY DETAILS MATTER

My own home is a fairly humble farmhouse in Yorkshire but I wanted to incorporate some of the details you might find in a grander house. In my bathroom, I used a grosgrain ribbon at the junction of the panelling and the wallpaper.

Like a river asserting its way through a landscape, the ribbon finds its path around the door, the window reveals and the marble upstand behind the sink. It has been pleated so it can twist and turn around the curved edges. It's a detail you'd find around a fireplace in the drawing room of a stately home, but it's here in my little bathroom and it still feels appropriate but so special. It gives me such pleasure to see it every day.

MARY GRAHAM

MANOR HOUSE

'Never let it be said that we can't do pared back,' Mary declares with a laugh. 'In fact, in some spaces here I think we've actually been quite spartan.' It's understandable why she and Nicole might want to make this point, because these aren't the first qualities that would come to mind when most people think of Salvesen Graham. But it was absolutely the right approach for this project, in a handsome, predominantly 19th-century country house in the East Midlands of England. And, of course, everything is relative – including the idea of 'pared back'. Because the rooms on the following pages still hum with energy and interest.

'What this house really needed was a gentle modernisation; not a complete reimagining of the space,' explains Nicole. It was being taken on by the next generation of the family with the client returning to the UK after living abroad. He wanted the house to retain the essence of the one he'd spent time in as a child, but to better reflect his life and tastes today.

This balancing act – preserving the best of the house's past without letting it get in the way of its evolution – is always a challenge both for the incoming generation and the interior designer. To achieve it was an exercise in editing as much as anything else. Although the impact Mary and Nicole's work had on the house was dramatic, it was all done with a light touch.

The house benefitted from being filled with beautiful paintings and furniture collected by the family and passed down over generations. These were thinned out and redistributed, given a new lease of life as they inhabited new rooms. 'The antiques were very good pieces, and we wanted to give them room to breathe, to be seen and celebrated,' Nicole says. An 18th-century burr wood armoire is found a new home in the drawing room; an upstairs landing feels more complete with a Georgian tripod table, now topped with a flower arrangement and piled with books. What is particularly successful, however, is the way that Mary and Nicole have in places teamed these antiques with contemporary pieces – modern icons of British design by the likes of Pinch, Max Rollitt and Soane Britain. And crucially, the juxtapositions created don't feel forced; the elegance never tips towards gimmickry.

All of this is played out against a relatively neutral backdrop. Most of the walls are painted in the lightest of greys, creams, greens and pinks. These are colours that look beautiful with rich brown furniture and gilt frames; they are shades that seem to encourage the light to flow across a room, because there is a lightness and airiness to this house. The uncluttered and slightly desaturated background also allows for a celebration of the interior architecture, from the curve or an archway or nook to the newly added, aubergine-backed bookcases in the study. And while it could never be described as minimal, there is an undeniable sense of spareness to the spaces.

Where a modern spirit has been expressed most strikingly is through the fabrics that Mary and Nicole used throughout the house. You can see it in the blue and white Bennison fabric and wallpaper in the guest loo, in curtains made in a bold red ikat from Le Manach and on lampshades in coral silk or marbled paper. And never underestimate the ability of mustard-coloured silk curtains and blinds to bring sunshine and positivity to a room. These choices were an important part in Mary and Nicole's armoury for freshening up otherwise quite traditional rooms.

This can be seen upstairs too, where simple, unfussy but deeply comfortable bedrooms are inhabited by a mixture of antiques and upholstered furniture against neutral-coloured backdrops. A triumph up here was the salvaging of the existing blue bathtub and sink which helped set the tone for the creamy parchment and forget-me-not blue colour palette which is also in the adjacent bedroom.

As well as pared back or restrained, I would add 'considered' to the list of adjectives to describe the designers' approach to this house. It requires real skill to create such an impression on an interior while conducting the lightest of interventions. It is an incredibly thoughtful approach.

ABOVE and LEFT: The study is a pared back space with artworks and simple furniture chosen to let the client's collection of antique books be the focus. OVERLEAF: Yellow silk soft furnishing bring the drawing room to life.

ABOVE and RIGHT: A hallway leading to a downstairs cloakroom and landing on the first floor are spaces defined by the choice of fabrics and wallpapers in bold colours and with distinctive large-scale patterns.

ABOVE and LEFT: The starting point for this bedroom and bathroom was the original sky blue bathtub that Mary and Nicole spotted on its way to the skip and saved from being thrown away. The rooms now combine the old with the new, pairing lacquer with mahogany, and stripes with scallops.

MANOR HOUSE

COLLECTED & CURATED

Arguably one of the worst things that happened to people's homes over the past few decades is what became, for some, an obsession with the idea of decluttering. It came about in the 1990s, around the same time that Ikea encouraged everyone to chuck out their chintz, so that we could all live more modern, streamlined lives. Suddenly, being surrounded by objects inherited, gathered, accumulated over years (and maybe needing a light dust) was deemed old-fashioned. 'But I think it's easy to forget the power of "things" and of being surrounded by objects that mean something to you,' says Mary. This must be one of the central tenets of English decorating.

What is a collected and curated interior? 'It's a space that feels authentic – like it has been pulled together over time,' explains Nicole. And it is something that is, at its best, deeply personal to the inhabitant of a space. 'Everyone has an interest or can have their interest piqued. It could be modern art or studio pottery or baseball caps. It might be travel. We always tell our clients that these are the elements that need to be reflected somewhere in their home – they will be so much happier in the space. And we're really excited about helping them discover what that might be.' They are firm believers of the 'only real rule' of Bunny Williams, doyenne of American decorating, that: 'if you love something it will work'. 'We'll make it work somewhere,' Mary says. 'We do see that as a challenge that we enjoy taking on.'

Mary and Nicole are not designers who come with a long list of red lines; they are not of the old-school decorator/dictator variety. But if there is one thing that breaks their hearts it is the prospect of filling a room from one of those one-stop home accessory shops that specialise in 'props' that pretend to be something they are not. You know the sort – the ones that sell mass-produced 'artisan' ceramics, faux 'antique' botanical prints; brand-new shabby chic. 'I'd rather a client have something small but meaningful that they won at a fun fair, or picked up on holiday – anything that they have a connection with,' says Nicole.

The reality is that sometimes Mary and Nicole do have to fake it. Or at least fake the time it has taken to achieve the collected and curated aesthetic. Because not everyone comes with a fully formed collection or even an idea of what it is that they want to surround themselves with. Not all houses already benefit from generations of accumulated objects that can be reassessed, reordered and rearranged. A second home or a pied-à-terre will often need a relatively quickly assembled layer of life's flotsam and jetsam to make them feel like a home. This is where the skill (and contacts) of the interior designer comes in.

Curating a shelf of objects, a series of surfaces in one room or a wall of pictures is about storytelling. And the narrative is that of the people who live there: their interests, their memories, their heritage. What Nicole and Mary leave space for though is room for that story to develop.

'The hope is that at the end of the process the client feels empowered to add to it themselves, to change it around,' says Nicole. 'We're setting them off on their own journey, and that's how the space will continue to reflect who they are.'

OBJECTS WITH MEANING

*As I write this I am looking at an antique
mahogany tea caddy in my kitchen. It isn't a
fine piece or anything special, but for me
it is a symbol of home.*

*My childhood home had one very similar
but we didn't keep tea in it; it's where we put
our keys. It was an ever-present feature in my
family's life, even when we moved house.*

*So, when my husband and I bought our first
house, my mother bought a tea caddy for us.
It was such a moment; I felt like a grown-up.
We keep our keys in it and our daughters are
growing up with it. I know I'll end up
buying one for them one day.*

NICOLE SALVESEN

MOUNTAIN HOME

When work prompted a young couple to relocate from California to Colorado, they saw it as an opportunity for change: it would be a completely different type of house, a new way of living. He is American; she is British and they wanted this project to have the very best qualities of both traditions: somewhere relaxed and comfortable, with a sense of elegance but without a bit of stuffiness.

Few of Mary and Nicole's projects in the UK are in buildings younger than 100 years old. Conversely, when it comes to houses in the United States and Canada, there aren't a huge number of centenarians, which was one of the reasons this one was so appealing to the designers.

The house is American Craftsman in style and part of a community of heritage homes dating back to the early 20th century. Nestled in the foothills of Colorado's Rocky Mountains, the house is constructed from brick and shiplap cladding with a veranda wrapping itself around from the front to the back. You could say there is a Norman Rockwell-esque charm to it. The many period features were rightfully protected, and as Nicole explains, 'these were to be enhanced and celebrated'.

'One of the real challenges was that a lot of the work was done in the early days of Covid,' explains Mary. This meant that the relationship between the designers and their clients was established via Zoom, a situation that was new to everyone. 'I have a distinct memory of our first meeting with the builder where he appeared on our screen wearing a Stetson, which we loved,' recalls Mary. For many expats, the pandemic suddenly made the world feel very big again; 'home' seemed far away, something that no doubt fed into the brief to add a layer of Englishness to this lovely example of architectural Americana.

'What we definitely weren't trying to do was make it a living museum of a 1900s' mining town house,' says Nicole. 'It was less about what would have been there, and more what felt appropriate'. A case in point is the entrance hall where the wallpaper has a small-scale pattern: a style that has a certain Victorian feel to it. The Arts and Crafts lantern looks like it might have had a previous life. And while the approach to the existing architecture and detailing was respectful, it wasn't reverential. For example, some of the original pine woodwork in the space was painted a sage green, a decision that subdued its slightly overwhelming orange tones. Now as the eye traverses the space, it can more easily take in and enjoy the beautiful craftsmanship of the unpainted sections.

Making an older house work for modern day life is always a balancing act. In this case, rather than opening up the rooms to create multifunctional spaces, the relatively formal structure of the layout was maintained. A library is a snug and cosy space, while the drawing room has a grown-up and sophisticated atmosphere. A boon to Nicole and Mary was how engaged the clients were in the process, and that can be seen in the collection of art that was amassed during the project.

Upstairs, the bedrooms (particularly the master suite) are layered with colour and pattern: florals and stripes, paisleys and soft geometrics conspire in a palette of pinks and greens. One exception is towards the back of the house in the more utilitarian Shaker-style kitchen. The colour play is gentler here, with the fitted units and large kitchen island painted different shades of blue.

Next door however, the energetic mix returns. The 'hearth room' is an informal dining space with windows on three sides. A striped floral fabric has been used for curtains and blinds and it works so well with the lines of the painted tongue-and-groove panelling added to the ceiling. Upholstered dining chairs, vintage rattan chairs and a built-in window seat painted a vibrant green all contribute to this layered aesthetic that Nicole and Mary are so adept at creating.

ABOVE and LEFT: There was some beautiful original wood in the hallways, but perhaps a little too much. Some of it was painted this restful sage green to make it a less dominating feature of the entrance to the home.

MOUNTAIN HOME

ABOVE and RIGHT: This central space in the house, which might have become neglected, serves as a hallway-cum-library that connects different rooms.

MOUNTAIN HOME

'Sometimes you have to lean into a room's greatest challenges. The awkward shape of a space can become its most appealing feature. Not every angle has to be perfectly square.'

MARY GRAHAM

ABOVE and LEFT: A staircase leading down to the basement and a nook just off the kitchen share the same fresh colour palette and pared back aesthetic. This repetition throughout a house helps to create a cohesive feeling.

'Don't be afraid to wallpaper irregular, angled walls: it can actually help unify and rationalise the space.'

NICOLE SALVESEN

UPSTAIRS DOWNSTAIRS

It doesn't matter how beautifully decorated a house is if it doesn't offer the practical solutions that you need or if the flow of the rooms doesn't feel right. 'People are usually more fixated on what the end result is going to look like,' says Nicole. 'And that's understandable. But we always stress the importance of getting the layout right first because it's going to have such an impact on their lives.' Finessing their planning drawings is an aspect that they enjoy working on and getting right.

Consider a house a little like an off-the-peg article of clothing: with a bit of nipping in, taking up or letting out, you should be able to achieve an exact fit. In the same way, the best interior design will tailor a house to the shape of your life. Salvesen Graham might suggest repositioning rooms or changing their function in ways that clients might not have envisaged. 'Sometimes it's a case of simply explaining that there are options,' she continues. 'We've definitely convinced people that they might be happier with fewer bedrooms, or a smaller bedroom, if it meant they could have a dressing room and a beautiful big bathroom.'

In recent decades, the idea of open-plan living has been one of the overarching trends determining how many people use their homes. And while Mary and Nicole agree that today's houses do usually need a large space where a family can gather and spend time, it's fair to say that 'open-plan' is not their default solution when it comes to creating these spaces. 'Open-plan and English decorating are not natural bedfellows,' concedes Mary. 'But that's not to say that you can't work with the idea of it.' You can see this most obviously in the way they design large, multifunctional kitchen spaces, where connected dining or seating areas have the impression of being separated through the use of devices, such as dwarf walls, steps or jib doors. And they are likely to make sure a floor plan also allows for other smaller rooms to which someone can retreat and close the door.

Most of the houses that they are commissioned to work on were designed and built at a time when people used their homes in a very different way. Generally, we live less formal lives than we did 100 or even 50 years ago though, call it the Downton Abbey effect, but clients with houses big and small and on both sides of the Atlantic, do still crave that slightly 'back of house' feel in the spaces that were once the reserve of domestic staff. A Shaker-style kitchen is a case in point, but it includes other traditionally 'service'-related parts of the house. That list includes a boot room, a utility room, a pantry and a laundry. 'A boot room for a family of surfers who need to hang wetsuits is a different proposition to a house that just needs some pegs for coats and a bench for someone to sit on while pulling off wellies,' says Mary. The plans they create are intensely thought out and practical. They are scenario-based schemes, where needs are anticipated and met.

THE IN-BETWEEN SPACES

There is a temptation when designing a new house or when renovating an old one, to create perfectly efficient spaces and iron out oddities. But I don't subscribe to Le Corbusier's idea that houses are 'machines for living'. In fact, we often find ourselves trying to add in slightly useless spaces; not every inch of space needs to be maximised.

There is so much to be said for creating breathing space. Maybe a half landing can just have a lovely pair of curtains rather than being transformed into an office. I like to see if there is a quiet moment to be created between a busy drawing room and a richly decorated dining room.

MARY GRAHAM

TOWNHOUSE

This handsome townhouse on a quiet street in London's Chelsea, home to a couple and their three children, is proof of how much can be achieved in a short period of time. It is also testament to the power of good decorating to create a dramatic impact in a space.

'This wasn't a building project,' Nicole explains. 'That was clear from the very beginning.' Their clients, who were relocating from California, had bought the five-floor Victorian house in July and needed to be in by September. 'This should have been a two-year project,' she continues. 'Yet it was done in three months.' What was required was excellent communication and trust between the designers and their client. 'And honesty,' Mary says. 'You have to be able to speak frankly with each other when decisions need to be made quickly.'

There was to be no structural work, nor architectural. That said, Mary and Nicole added some previously removed architectural detailing, which is most noticeable in the entrance hall. The space is surprisingly bright, with a gentle palette of blues and greens enhanced by plenty of natural light. The new square panelling establishes the soft geometry of the space where a small-scale patterned wallpaper creeps all the way up to the top floor, while a runner woven in a playful herringbone pattern climbs the stairs. It is unusual for the entrance hall of a London terraced house to feel surprising or delightful, but this one is both.

In fact, playful was one of the briefs the clients set Mary and Nicole. 'The idea of how the children would live in the house and interact with it was a driving force,' explains Mary. 'The clients wanted us to create a sense of magic and wonder.' Open any door off the patterned hallway and the staircase that creeps up the house and you discover more intriguing details. In the downstairs bathroom, a hand-painted floral motif climbs up the walls and onto the ceiling. It is indeed magical.

Back on the ground floor is the classic double reception room of London terraced houses. It was originally two rooms and is a notoriously awkward space to make work for modern living. Nicole and Mary treated it as a single, connected room, with one half acting as a grown-up drawing room while the other is a clever hybrid, serving as somewhere for the children to play at the table, a library or an intimate dining area. The owners are enthusiastic and very knowledgeable art collectors, so here, as in virtually every area of the house, an interesting mixture of good contemporary and 20th-century artworks hangs alongside more decorative pieces. 'It helped that we knew these rooms would have brilliant art to help finish them off so in a way we were creating a backdrop for it,' says Nicole.

The house feels remarkably established for somewhere created in such a short period of time. Much of that is achieved through the decorative details: the layering of fabrics, patterns, textures and artwork, and in some rooms the grosgrain trim that edges its way around the space. That said, some of the design decisions were based on the reality that this might not be the family's forever home. 'They had to make the decision to buy this house fairly quickly, and they knew that perhaps one day they would move,' explains Mary. 'That was another reason this was primarily a decorative project.'

It also explains why the house isn't filled with unavoidably expensive new fitted joinery. 'The idea of decorating a room that's only going to last a couple of years doesn't sit well with us,' she says. As such there is plenty of free-standing storage that can come with them when they do decide to leave, including modern, bespoke dressers in the drawing room and a smart library shelf in the adjoining room.

A sort of 'masculine femininity' could be considered a Salvesen Graham signature, where floral fabrics are offset by sludgy or muted colourways, skirted furniture is counterbalanced by more tailored pieces and pretty details are used alongside more structured, tailored lines. The drawing room gathered fabrics sit against a tobacco backdrop, in the hallway geometrics meet florals, and even in the kitchen, chintz sits alongside joinery. In the main bedroom, a fully dressed four-poster bed and pleated lampshades are 'oomphed up with rich inky colours like aubergine and dark blue,' as Mary puts it. The contrast really is the distinctive element that Mary and Nicole bring to a project.

LEFT: A small-scale wallpaper extends up the staircase to the second floor. ABOVE: A small study, which had tongue-and-groove panelling added to the walls, is at the end of the entrance hall for which new half-height panelling was designed. PREVIOUS: The elegant drawing room is a comfortable mix of colour and pattern.

ABOVE and RIGHT: The back of a classic 'double reception' room typical of London's terraced houses has been turned into a multifunctional space used for reading, playing games and intimate suppers. OVERLEAF: Family meals in the kitchen take place surrounded by art, antiques and floral fabrics.

ABOVE and RIGHT: An example of how Salvesen Graham layers colours and patterns, not only within a room but also within spaces that are visually connected.

ABOVE and LEFT: Contemporary art, lacquered furniture and classic 'county house' elements work together to create an eclectic look in the main bedroom.

TOWNHOUSE

ABOVE and RIGHT: Wallpaper and fabrics from Salvesen Graham's own collection (even on the lampshades) create a cohesive – and very pretty – effect in a child's bedroom.

ABOVE and LEFT: A more European influence can be detected in another child's room where the impression of a tented ceiling has been artfully created with grosgrain ribbon.

'Children's rooms don't have to be childish. Choosing a more sophisticated palette can help a room evolve and grow with the child.'

MARY GRAHAM

ANTIQUES

Mary and Nicole aren't designers that come with a set of 'non-negotiables', but you get the sense that antiques come pretty high on their list of must-haves when they are devising a scheme. 'Antiques have a way of anchoring or giving weight to a room,' explains Mary. This might be in a physical sense – if it's a large piece of furniture or something with a real presence. 'But more often than not, it's the feeling of history that comes with them and gives the piece substance.' For what is English decorating, particularly in the country house tradition, without the suggestion of an earlier time or the appearance (even if contrived) of accumulation over generations?

While the pair have an appreciation for fine or unique examples, and have happily worked with such pieces in clients' collections, their approach to antiques tends to come from a more decorative point of view. 'It's easy to have a very narrow view of what an antique is, but the joy of them is the variety they offer,' says Mary. 'From a French polished piece with gilding or marquetry details, to a rustic armoire or something a little more elegant from the Regency period, it is such a wide spectrum.' They are firm believers that there is an antique out there for anybody.

Nancy Lancaster is credited as saying that: 'To put very fine pieces of furniture in a room that is without architectural distinction is as absurd as wearing a tiara with a bathing suit.' But what is particularly appealing about Mary and Nicole's approach is their relaxed attitude to what a purist might find 'appropriate' in a space. And that's interesting, because when working in a historical context, it's very important to them to pay close attention to what is architecturally appropriate. There's a little more wiggle room when it comes to antiques. To some extent, it's about what 'feels' right.

Salvesen Graham is more than happy to combine pieces from different eras; in fact, it is usually their default. And when they have clients who come to a project with a houseful of antiques that they might not want or know what to do with, the pair are quick to suggest a redistribution of pieces into new rooms. 'Working with antiques is often about curation,' Nicole says. 'And making them work for a 21st-century home rather than creating a museum.' A television can be housed in an old cabinet that has been adapted for the purpose; the 'oppressiveness' of a collection of mahogany furniture in a dining room might be diluted by spreading the pieces more widely around the house. Antique textiles are brought in to add interest and a unique element.

Antiques, while not always the stars of the show in a room, add a sense of permanence and timelessness that is hard to create with a new piece of furniture. They also tell a story. 'A little table might remind you of what your grandmother had in her house,' says Nicole. 'Or perhaps you remember sitting on your grandfather's knee in a not terribly attractive chair that you've now inherited. There can be space for these pieces; there should be space for them; it's just a matter of weaving them into a space and into the narrative of a room.' That's part of the magic in what Salvesen Graham does so well.

A NEW LOVE AFFAIR

Like many people, I discovered the thrill of online auctions during one of the pandemic lockdowns. And so began an obsession — a new love affair — with Masons ironstone jugs.

These aren't fine antiques; ironstone was developed in the 19th century as a cheaper alternative to porcelain. But they are so beautiful and quirky and weird, with Japanese floral motifs and handles shaped like serpents' tails. And they're practical — they make great little jugs for flowers. There are so many things you can accumulate in this world, but to find something lovely but also useful is so satisfying. So is the discovery that you can develop a passion for something a little later in life.

MARY GRAHAM

ARTS & CRAFTS

A handsome Georgian rectory is what many people might picture when imagining a house in the countryside: symmetrical and in proportion; a rational layout; easy to decorate and fill with life. That was not the reality facing the couple who bought this house in Hampshire a few years ago, however. Instead, they fell in love with a house that was a hodgepodge of different periods and styles. It's not hard to see why the owners were charmed: set in a pretty hamlet, the house has views over farmland and woodland for as far as the eye can see. Nor is it difficult to understand why they asked Nicole and Mary to help them make sense of it for them and their three sons.

The house has had at least three phases of construction: early 17th century, mid-19th century, and late 20th century. 'And each period was so noticeably different,' recalls Nicole. 'Dark, low ceilings were next to very light spaces, there were rooms that felt like a cottage, and a modern kitchen that had a silver pole in it, reminiscent of pole dancing.' Nicole and Mary's task was to create a sense of harmony between the various spaces. 'It was about tying it all together, while still letting every room have its identity and character,' says Mary.

The entrance hall is a wide, handsome space with panelling covering most of the walls and an impressive wooden staircase. 'The wood had been mistreated for years and was too dark, with too much patina,' explains Nicole. It was soon cleaned up into the rich, honey-toned hue we see today, which, in a way, helped establish the colour scheme for the rest of the home. 'Because there was so much wood, we went for a palette that was a bit earthier and warmer than people might expect in a period house,' Mary says.

The predominant colour in the drawing room is a pale rose-pink, prevented from becoming too saccharine by teaming it with shots of raspberry, a touch of leopard print, a pair of armchairs in tobacco-coloured linen and a thick rush matting carpet that anchors the space. 'It was one of those rooms that when we first walked in, we could immediately picture how it could look,' recalls Nicole.

Less obvious was what to do in the dining room, which is directly off the entrance hall and shares the same wood panelling. It also has an ornate, Tudor-style plaster ceiling. Despite these historic and slightly heavy architectural elements, it feels remarkably fresh and modern. This is in no small part thanks to the panelling being painted a muted, light green. 'It's not something we would normally have done, but it stops the room feeling like a gentlemen's club,' says Mary. 'And instead of some dark space in the middle of the house it has become a room that you could just as happily be in for lunch as dinner.'

Although it doesn't come across as such when you visit the house, upon reflection there is a lot of decoration and use of layering. 'It was through colour and fabrics that we could create a softness and harmony that meant you didn't feel as though you were jumping around,' Nicole says.

The kitchen and adjoining breakfast room are a case in point. This is a big space and an important part of the house, but it needed to feel warm and inviting. 'Somewhere three boys could be fed and their friends entertained,' Mary explains. They covered the walls in grass cloth which immediately gave it a domestic rather than a utilitarian feel. There are blinds in pretty fabrics. The breakfast room – formerly an orangery with multiple gothic arched windows – has been completely reimagined. Today it has a farm-house feel, and not just because of the slightly simple country furniture sitting on top of an antique rug: the gothic arches were squared off; heavy white-washed beams were added to the ceiling and a fireplace was installed at one end. As Nicole puts it, these clever architectural tricks, 'bring the room back into the house rather than it feeling like an extension which runs into the garden.'

What has been achieved is remarkable. Salvesen Graham hasn't changed the essence of the house; it is still a building comprised of distinct parts. And those transitional spaces that mark the evolution of the house are still visible. What's different is that they have been softened and blended, giving it a sense of harmony.

ABOVE and RIGHT: Mary and Nicole always stress the importance of getting 'back of house' spaces right – and not only in terms of how they function. These utilitarian spaces are rich in decorative detail.

'Kitchens aren't just somewhere to cook. They are places that people gravitate to, to spend time in – together or on their own. It's important to create the space to make this possible.'

NICOLE SALVESEN

ABOVE and RIGHT: The wall panelling in the dining room, with its beautiful Tudoresque plaster ceiling, was painted to give it a less formal feel.

ABOVE and LEFT: A back hall and one of the two studies are two slightly more cottagey spaces in what is actually a substantial house, in contrast to the drawing room (overleaf) which feels architecturally very different and far grander.

ARTS & CRAFTS

ABOVE, LEFT and OVERLEAF: The master suite is a linear enfilade of spaces at the rear of the house overlooking the garden. Sandwiched between the bedroom and bathroom is the dressing room with Salvesen Graham's signature trimming detail around the walls.

ARTS & CRAFTS

PATTERN

If it were to be said that Nicole and Mary have developed a language for the way that Salvesen Graham designs, their skill for using pattern would undoubtedly be their signature. It is certainly something for which they have become known. A tradition for a particular way of combining and layering patterns is also one of the defining elements of English decorating.

Empire, 18th-century grand tourism and 19th-century global trade, all played their role in the evolution of the English Country House style. And this is especially evident in the fabrics found in these houses. They come from all over the world and draw on the traditions, skills and motifs of the respective regions and cultures from which they originate. Paisleys and chintzes from India have long been the mainstay of sophisticated drawing rooms; Persian and Turkish rugs have been rolled out in elegant bedrooms of smart houses for centuries; the walls of opulent dining rooms continue to be covered in scenic hand-painted silks from China. 'It's interesting how you need to have these different elements in a room or throughout a home to feel properly "English",' Nicole muses. Perhaps a more recent addition to this eclectic collection of styles is the 20th-century Swedish textiles which Salvesen Graham will often include to add a fresher, more contemporary feel.

In the chapter *Working with Colour*, Nicole and Mary mentioned what they call the 'hero fabric' of their schemes. 'These are patterned fabrics that act as a starting point for a room,' Mary explains. 'They are chosen because of the potential they offer a room, or because they completely capture the imagination of the client and are something they absolutely love.' In the final room, the fabric won't necessarily be the star of the show; it might end up on a fireplace fender or just a cushion. Its influence might not immediately be seen on the fabric choices for the curtains, the ottoman and the armchairs, but the way that these elements blend together will create a feeling of cohesion. 'I think it's what makes a room comfortable,' says Nicole.

The key for Salvesen Graham is to find an element within that hero fabric that can be drawn out, repeated or referenced in the secondary fabric choices. 'It might be a colour, a motif, or even a texture,' Nicole explains. 'You can spin it out into so many different directions then, but there will be something tying it all together'.

Working with such diverse source materials requires confidence. 'Not only a confidence to get it "right",' comments Mary. 'Because you don't want a room to be too perfect or too coordinated.' Part of the beauty of the mixture of these patterns is often in the element that slightly throws things 'off'. 'When you have a beautiful French floral on a bed, a Chinoiserie on the walls and a paisley throw all working together in harmony, that's when you know you can throw in a less obviously beautiful or even ugly needlepoint footstool and it can be incredibly chic,' says Nicole.

For clients who might not yet have the confidence to do something particularly bold or who simply have a more understated style, Mary and Nicole will express their love of pattern though more muted or even tonal shades, with a combination of weaves and textures or with a patterned plain. 'Working with pattern doesn't have to be dazzling and intense, it can be calming and subtle,' Mary insists. 'In either case, it's an exciting element to have in a scheme, and so much fun to be able to empower clients to use it and enjoy living with it.'

THE POWER OF PATTERN

I have been a pattern person since I was a small child, whether in the clothes I wear or interiors. Perhaps as I've grown up and become a designer I've learned to dial it down a bit; that's a natural journey.

But I've also seen the power of pattern to completely transform any room. It instantly adds interest and layers to a space with not a lot going on, and conversely, it creates the perfect backdrop for personal elements — the photos and accessories that clients will usually bring to a room.

Pattern isn't about frivolous decoration; it can be really practical. In a busy family home, a floral sofa will be far more forgiving with mess and stains than a plain one. And a little pattern might be just the thing to 'enhance' that slightly challenging but much loved ornament from your child's art class...

NICOLE SALVESEN

GEORGIAN HOUSE

The story of this house, on the edge of a small village near Windsor, is one of identifying and achieving potential. 'I remember how excited we were the first time we visited,' Nicole recalls. 'We could immediately see how we could help make it not only more aesthetically pleasing, but also much nicer to live in.' Roll the clock back 50-odd years, however, and it was the potential visit of Jackie Onassis that inspired a previous owner to add some glamour to the house by laying acres of red carpet. Another former custodian of the house created a 'Jacuzzi room'. These possibly misguided, and definitely outdated, elements were still in situ when Nicole and Mary's clients bought the house. The young couple and their two children had lived there without making any changes for around five years before bringing the designers on board. They'd realised the house was ready to have its potential unleashed.

A rethink of the layout was what was most needed. The main part of the house dates back to 1765 but later additions created a building that was long and thin. 'It was impossible to get from one end to the other without walking through rooms to get to other rooms,' says Mary. Because of its protected status, the clients had worked with an architect to obtain planning permission to remove a staircase from the original entrance hall and create a double-height hallway adjacent to this, with new stairs leading up to a gallery landing. Architectural purists might not have agreed with the decision to do so, but it was obvious how the change added to the house, not least in the way the spaces flowed. 'The challenge then was to make sure we got the architectural detailing right, so that it felt historic and correct.' They enlisted the help of a regular collaborator, the architect Rupert Cunningham, a director at Ben Pentreath.

One of the greatest transformations in this house can be seen in a space that wasn't part of the initial brief: the original 18th-century gabled chapel. 'It was freezing cold, had no heating and was full of gym equipment,' recalls Nicole. Maybe the clients thought it was beyond redemption, but it certainly captured the imagination of the designers. 'We told them we'd make it into an amazing dining room for them,' she continues. 'And yes, we'd make it warm.' Now, with walls lined in red painted hessian, it is a completely uplifting space that is illuminated during the day through its large Gothic window and by night via an oversized chandelier that hangs above the table.

The client wanted something colourful and fun – a reflection of the family. 'She's artistic and vibrant as a person,' explains Mary. 'And definitely didn't want it to feel like a stuffy English country house.' But with a husband and two sons, it's no wonder she responded eagerly to the colour pink, which appears in various shades in many of the rooms.

A suite of four rooms was created upstairs for the couple, thanks to the rejigging of the staircase downstairs. It's a grown-up, sophisticated space to spend time in, slightly separated from the children's and guest bedrooms on the other side of the new gallery landing.

There are fun, light-hearted and more modern elements in this house though, and appropriately so for a young family. A wallpaper featuring a menagerie of polar bears and tigers cover the walls of a downstairs loo, while an energetic Joseph Frank floral fabric was used to cover the L-shaped sofa in the family room. The ottoman in the drawing room is covered in a custom-made geometric needlepoint textile in a kaleidoscope of colours. It sets the tone for a room that is far more relaxed than many of its type.

And then there is the bar, a room that didn't exist until the very end of the project. Just off the dining room, it is a joyful space, with cabinets painted a mid-century modern shade of green and walls papered in a large-scale flamestitch wallpaper by Fromental, recoloured by Salvesen Graham in uplifting shades of pink, yellow, green and blue. It's no surprise that it has become one of the couple's favourite spaces in the house.

ABOVE and LEFT: The components of a relatively traditional kitchen are presented in block colours in a contemporary palette, giving it a fresh, modern spirit, while the family room (previous page) off the kitchen is an extension of this palette, including the scallop rug designed by Mary and Nicole for Jennifer Manners.

ABOVE and LEFT: Although it has all the elements of a formal drawing room, at the client's request the space has a far more relaxed feel, thanks to the fabrics and some of the punchier colour choices.

GEORGIAN HOUSE

'Using the same colour on the walls, joinery and architectural detailing is a way of adding harmony to a room with lots going on.'

MARY GRAHAM

LEFT and ABOVE: The utility room is a hardworking space with decorative flourishes, including scallop-edge detailing on the panelling and a pretty skirted work surface. The blue-green of the woodwork is continued into the little downstairs loo which has pretty tiles and wallpaper.

GEORGIAN HOUSE

ABOVE: The design for this bar is all about fun, with a striking flame stitch design used on the wall, gathered skirt, Roman blind and even the lampshade. RIGHT: In the downstairs loo, an equally bold and witty de Gournay wallcovering has been used.

GEORGIAN HOUSE

LEFT: Salvesen Graham's Great Check fabric is expertly layered with florals, paisleys and other large- and small-scale patterns in the main bedroom. ABOVE: Great Check can be seen again here holding its own in a guest bedroom.

GEORGIAN HOUSE

'Bathrooms are places with lots of hard surfaces and finishes, so they can definitely take some prettier elements if you want something a little softer.'

NICOLE SALVESEN

THE COLLECTION

These days it is very much de rigueur for an interior designer to have their own product line. It is an obvious way for a studio to offer an alternative gateway to its offering. But to speak with Mary and Nicole about The Collection by Salvesen Graham is to understand that it is more than simply a brand extension. In fact, it is an extension of their entire approach to design and decoration: a combination of the useful and the beautiful, something rooted in the historic but with a clearly modern spirit, and innately and indelibly English.

You can really see this in one of the most impressive and fastest growing parts of the collection: fabrics and wallpapers that take inspiration from archive documents that largely take inspiration from early 18th century designs. These simplified designs capture the essence of the originals but have been refined and recoloured in a fresh and usable palette. 'What was important for us was that they maintained that connection with the past but felt right for right now,' explains Mary. 'That way they could fit well within a traditional interior filled with antiques or a very spartan modern environment where the focus is all about individual pieces.'

Whether on fabrics or other items, there are simple, classic motifs: a familiar floral or sprig of leaves, a bamboo cane, a Greek key, the column, a scalloped edge. As individual pieces, they carry the same DNA as a Salvesen Graham project; as a whole, they will sit together comfortably in countless permutations to create any number of ready-made schemes. 'Realistically, no one needs yet another fabric collection from an interior design studio,' Mary admits. 'But we set out with a mission to view The Collection holistically, based on our experience as decorators, and to create designs that were really useful and complementary, and that felt comfortable and natural together.'

Their first venture into product design was an elegant armchair in collaboration with the upholstered furniture specialist David Seyfried. It proved such a success that it has since been developed into a range that includes a sofa, ottoman, window seat and more. And it also whetted the designers' appetite for developing their own collection.

With the exception of the rug specialist Jennifer Manners, who has her rugs woven by artisans in Nepal and India, all of the producers that Nicole and Mary work with are based in England. This of course serves a practical purpose as it means they are able to collaborate closely with the various workshops they partner with up and down the country. Dining chairs are made in Kent; side tables and trays in Yorkshire; fabrics and wallpapers are printed in Leicestershire; the woven fabrics are produced in Suffolk. Passementerie is made in collaboration with the British fabric heritage brand Sanderson, and produced in Loughborough.

'So much of what we do is about human connections,' Nicole says. 'And we've spent a lot of time getting to know the people who are making our pieces.' It has also been important for them to work with the best craftspeople available. 'There is such a disconnection with how and where things are made, and by whom,' Mary says. 'But we know our clients love to hear about the specialist skills that go into the creation of their homes. By continuing to work with these artisans we are helping to keep these specialist skills alive.'

NEVER STOP LEARNING

Learning new things makes you flex your creative muscles, and ultimately that's what makes you a better designer.

A few years ago, my husband and I bought a chalet in France — somewhere to ski in the winter and hike in the summer. But what I was most looking forward to was the chance to work on a completely different type of house; to see how Salvesen Graham could be interpreted in a 1990s' alpine building.

Our international clients come to us because of our 'English' aesthetic but this isn't always straightforward when you're working with architecture that isn't English — my own home in France and our international projects are a great chance to experiment with finishes and details to create that feeling in a way that was convincing, but also appropriate.

NICOLE SALVESEN

ACKNOWLEDGEMENTS

It is with huge gratitude that we thank our publisher, Kate Pollard, for coming to us with the idea of what became such a fulfilling project. Thank you for your patience as we learned the complex art of book publishing. Kate introduced us to Roger Barnard, the designer of this book, who we thank for his beautiful curation of our work.

He had great material to work with though, thanks to the photographers whose images light up the pages of this book: Simon Brown, Simon Upton, Alex James and Chris Horwood, in particular. As designers, it is always interesting (and sometimes nerve-wracking) to see how other creatives interpret your work. We always felt in safe hands with them.

To David Nicholls, who we asked to write this book: it has been a complete joy. You have captured the spirit of Salvesen Graham beautifully and we have loved this journey with you.

From our wonderful team, we'd like to single out the amazing Amy Eriksson for heartfelt thanks. You've been with us every step of the way, supporting us and carrying out countless tasks associated with the book, all with unwavering dedication and enthusiasm.

Our greatest thanks and appreciation go to our friends and families, particularly husbands Tom Salvesen and Sam Graham, who have been the most loyal supporters and champions of Salvesen Graham since day one. (And recently proofreaders too!) To our children, Genevieve, Romily and Margot Salvesen, and Beatrice and Laurie Graham: thank you for being your wonderful selves and for continuing to inspire us – and for understanding when sometimes we miss bedtime…

– Mary Graham and Nicole Salvesen

David Nicholls has written about international design and decoration for 25 years. Born and raised on the west coast of Canada, he moved to the United Kingdom in 1994, where he studied English Language and Literature at King's College, London. Early in his career, he worked at the Daily Telegraph serving as The Telegraph Magazine's design editor for more than a decade. David has curated exhibitions, served as a judge for industry awards and acted as advisor to design studios and brands. In 2015, he joined House & Garden magazine where he is currently its deputy editor. He lives in south London with his incredibly patient partner, Claudio.

Every reasonable effort has been made to acknowledge the copyright of artworks in this volume. Any errors or omissions that may have occurred are inadvertent and will be corrected in subsequent editions provided notification is sent in writing to the publisher.

PHOTOGRAPHY
Bond, Jonathan: 251 top left; 252 top left.
Brown, Simon: 8; 34 top left, top right; 67 top left; 95 top left, bottom right; 100-121; 123 top left; 124 bottom; 143 top right, bottom left, bottom right; 144 bottom; 148-169; 171 top right; 200 top right; 225 top left; 230-250.
Horwood, Chris: 2-3; 14-31; 33 bottom left; 67 top right, bottom right; 68 top right, bottom left, bottom right; 72-93; 95 top right, bottom left; 96 top left, top right; 123 top right, bottom left, bottom right; 124, top left, top right; 143 bottom right; 171 top left; 172 top right, bottom right; 176-197; 199 top left, top right, bottom left; 204-223; 225 bottom left; 226 top left, bottom left, bottom right; 251 top right, bottom left, bottom right; 254; Back Cover.
James, Alex: 34 bottom; 226 top right.
Seventy7: 252 bottom.
Sinclair, Michael © 2019 Christie's Images: 199 bottom right; 200 top left.
Smith, Rachael: 128-141; 200 bottom left.
Spring, Sophia: 7; 252 top right; 255.
Upton, Simon: Front Cover; 4; 11; 33 top left, top right, bottom right; 38-65; 67 bottom left; 68 top left; 96, bottom; 143 top left: 144 top left, top right: 171 bottom: 172, top left, bottom left; 200 bottom right; 225 top right, bottom right;

ARTISTS' WORKS
Ackermann, R.: titles unknown, dates unknown, (prints): 249.
Arp, Hans: *Affiche St. Gallen III*, 1966: 194.
Bill, Max: *Hard Line*, date unknown: 189, 226 top left.
Blackwell, Su: *Insects and Flowers*, 2022: 18 bottom left.
Boxer, Kate: *I won't eat you*, date unknown: 111; *Blue Wolf*, date unknown: 116.
Brandt, Gitte: *Le Léopard*, date unknown, (both prints): 120, 234-5.
Braque, Georges: *L'oiseau Jaune*, 1958 (print): 79 bottom.
Bruce High Quality Foundation: *Ray's Famous Original Oil Painting*, date unknown: 179 middle left, 181.
Cameron, Seth: *Tips (Spread)*, 2016: 185 right.
Cole, Lottie: *Writer's Retreat – Interior with Elisabeth Frink*, date unknown: 20; *T.S. Eliot, Four Quartets*, 2023: 68 top right; *Interior with Dutch Swag & Anonymous Woman*, 2022: 72, 75; *Derek Walker, Sea Canes*, 2024: 80; *Stephen Spender from The Truly Great*, 2024: 82, 84; *Interior with Young Girl Reading I*, 2024: 91; *Interior with Winifred Nicholson and Labradors*, date unknown: 200 top right.
Cory Wright, Harry: *Field 541*, 2022: 18 top left; *St Enedoc Church*, 2018: 240-241.
di Stefano, Arturo: *Santo Spirito*, 2013: 34 bottom.
Donnelly, Anne: *Hens with their Young*, 2002: 79 top.
Fairfax, Annabel: *Fruit and Flowers I, date unknown*: 217, right, above fireplace.
Feldmeyer, Nicolas: *Estate 1*, 2018: 158, 159.
Friend, Kate: *Piet Oudolf, Meconopsis Cambrica, Hummelo, Netherlands*, 2022 (postcard): 183.
Graham, Sarah: *Magnolia Painting III*, 2022: 151, 153.
Grenville, Hugo: *Still Life with Nude*, date unknown: 123 top right.
Guinness, Hugo: various: 143, 154 (all).
Hales, Michael: *Fata Morgana*, date unknown: 77.
Harman, Kevin: *Along Came Magnificence*, 2019: 21.
Harrison, Colin: *Farewell Marguerite Duras*, date unknown: 85.
Hart Dyke, James: *Marching Through Time* (top), 2022 and *Trees at Brancaster Staithe, Norfolk* (bottom), 2020: 14,199 top left.
Henderson, Nicholas: *Bathers*, date unknown: 226 bottom right.
Hopton, Georgie: *Pieces of Silver*, 2019: 29.
Iglesias Peco, Patricia: *Scroll*, date unknown: 186-187.
Jack, Robina: *earthenware plates*, date unknown: 117.
James, Ann-Marie: *After Dürer 29*, 2018: 166; *After Dürer 36*, 2018: 167.
Kanica: *Le Bal Géométrique XVI*, 2023: 78.
Lamb, Chloe: title unknown, date unknown: 11; *No Surprise* (top), 2022 and *Summer Square* (bottom), date unknown: 18, 95 top right; title unknown, date unknown: 143 bottom left, middle.
Lansley, Bridget: *Shades of Blue*, date unknown: 212-213.
Le Brun, Christopher: *Ideas of March IV*, 2019: 22.
Levine, Chris: *Equanimity* (part of a series) Jubilee Edition, 2022: 21.
Mackley, Evan: *A Pot of Spring*, date unknown: 243.
McEwen, Rory: *Old Carnations and Pinks*, date unknown, (prints): 86 top left.
Mrozowski, Ryan: *Untitled (Split Painting)*, 2024: 96 top left, 122 bottom right, 191.
Mühl, Roger: *Printemps*, 1972: 7, 179 bottom centre.
Ogawa, Kazumasa: *Japanese Flower Studies*, c. 1896, (prints): 182 left wall.
Park, Stuart: *Geraniums*, date unknown: 190 top.

Pomeroy, Richard: *collection of vessels*, date unknown: 14, 17.
Powell, Jemma: *Making Sandcastles*, date unknown: 216 top; *Little Group*, date unknown: 216 bottom.
Rathsmann, Birgit: *Hurricane (Bertha)*, date unknown: 182 right wall.
Rist, Pipilotti: *Sonnenaufgang im Land der untergehenden Sonne*, 1999: 179 bottom right, 181.
Rudd, Sam: *Country Walk*, date unknown: 96 top right.
Saito, Kiyoshi: *Winter in Aizu*, date unknown: 179 top right.
Stella, Joseph: *Cut Flowers*, date unknown: 77 bottom right,184.
Stettner, Luke: *The Single Monument (Circle)*, 2014: 7, 179 bottom left, 181.
Tatebayashi, Kaori: *Helleborus niger*, 2022: 25.
Walbeoffe, Sophie: title unknown, date unknown: 246 bottom.
Walter, Stephen: *London Subterranea*, 2012, (print): 8, 238.
Warhol, Andy: *Ingrid Bergman with Hat*, 1983: 123 top left.
West, Jennifer: *Shred the Gnar Full Moon Film Noir Frames 1*, 2014, (print): 188.
Wilson, Fred: *Best Man*, 2015: 190 bottom.

SALVESEN GRAHAM FABRICS
Zig Zag Stripe, Moss, 12-13.
Floral Sprig, Meadow, 36-37.
Floral Trail, Caramel, 70-71.
Great Check, Mustard, 98-99.
Zig Zag Stripe, Midnight, 126-127.
Genevieve, Endpapers, 146-147.
Floral Trail, Delicate, 174-175.
Little Check, Moss, 202-203.
Floral Border Stripe, Raspberry, 228-229.

Our heartfelt and extended thanks to our wonderful team of collaborators who help bring to life our design, from concept to creation. Architects and contractors, curtain makers, upholsterers and art consultants. Every project requires a huge team effort, thank you all.

Quadrille, Penguin Random House UK, One Embassy Gardens, 8 Viaduct Gardens, London SW11 7BW

Quadrille Publishing Limited is part of the Penguin Random House group of companies whose addresses can be found at *global.penguinrandomhouse.com*

Copyright © David Nicholls 2024

Salvesen Graham has asserted their right to be identified as the author of this Work in accordance with the Copyright, Designs and Patents Act 1988

No part of this book may be used or reproduced in any manner for the purpose of training artificial intelligence technologies or systems. In accordance with Article 4(3) of the DSM Directive 2019/790, Penguin Random House expressly reserves this work from the text and data mining exception.

Published by Quadrille in 2025
www.penguin.co.uk

A CIP catalogue record for this book is available from the British Library

ISBN 978-1-78488-963-0
10 9 8 7 6 5 4 3

Publishing Director Kate Pollard
Editor Imogen Fortes
Designer Roger Barnard
Production Manager Martina Georgieva

Colour reproduction by p2d

Printed in China by C&C Offset Printing Co., Ltd.

The authorised representative in the EEA is Penguin Random House Ireland, Morrison Chambers, 32 Nassau Street, Dublin D02 YH68.

Penguin Random House is committed to a sustainable future for our business, our readers and our planet. This book is made from Forest Stewardship Council® certified paper.